FU

G000075224

Published by: Cross Media Ltd.
13 Berners Street, London W1T 3LH, UK
Tel: 020-7436-1960 Fax: 020-7436-1930

Copyright of Photography and Text © Cross Media Ltd. 2001

Project Manager: Kazuhiro Marumo
Editor: J.L.Rollinson
Designer: Misa Watanabe
Photographer: Naomi Igawa, Hiroshi Mitani
Recipes: Nobuko Motohashi
Chef: Miyoko Yoshimura (Akasha Cooking School)
Coordinator: Masahiko Goto. Thanks to: Akasha Tōkōdō & Sono Aoki

ISBN 1-897701-77-2
Printed in Japan

All about tofu

The food that promotes healthy longevity

Tofu originated in China around 200 BC and was introduced to Japan in about 600 AD, and the making of different tofu has developed almost as an art form over this long history. It was originally the food of aristocrats, noblemen and monks, highly regarded as 'the food for a long, healthy life,' as those who were the healthiest and lived longest were indeed either monks, who ate it as a part of their vegetarian diet, or wealthy people who enjoyed substantial amounts of tofu as a luxury. By the 1500's however, the population at large adopted tofu into their diet, and by the late 1700's tofu cookery books were best-sellers. Nowadays in Japan, tofu is one of the most common ingredients and features in many everyday meals. It is has been scientifically proven that tofu contains good quality protein, is highly nutritious and low in calories.

Tofu and nutrition

Tofu can reduce cholesterol

All the nutrition of soya beans in a neat block of tofu

Tofu is made from the milk of ground soya beans.
The protein required by the body is made up of particular amino acids, and the protein in soya beans provides amino acids that are most closely aligned with the body's needs. As tofu is very easily digested it allows the body to make good use of these amino acids quickly and effectively, nourishing blood and muscle in a very balanced way.
Unsaturated fatty acids (linoleic acid) are effective in reducing cholesterol, and linoleic acid makes up 80% of the fat in soya beans, making tofu an almost essential ingredient for those concerned about heart related disease.

Tofu is gentle on the stomach

Anything that might inhibit digestion is removed naturally during the process of making tofu. This makes the protein and unsaturated fats easily digestible. It is possible to absorb 95% of the protein content of tofu, which is markedly higher than for other soya bean products. As tofu is so easy on the stomach it is very good for babies, the elderly and during periods of illness.

Tofu is gentle on the bowel

Despite the fact that tofu contains almost no fibre at all, it does have various useful elements that aid digestion. It contains oligosaccharides, which increase the amount of the helpful bifidobacteria in the gut. These bacteria contain a highly effective metabolising enzyme that prevents constipation and lowers blood pressure. As tofu is such a mild product it is very suitable for anyone with bowel trouble and is a healthy choice for those seeking to lose weight.

	TOFU 100g	CHICKEN 100g	FILLET STEAK 100g
calories	73kcal / 304kJ	218kcal / 910kJ	188kcal / 791kJ
protein	8.1g	26.3g	29.1g
fat	4.2g	12.5g	8.0g
-saturated	0.6g	3.4g	3.6g
-mono-unsat'd	1.0g	5.7g	3.2g
-poly-unsat'd	2.5g	2.4g	0.5g
cholesterol	0	110mg	71mg
vitamin E	0.95mg	0.21mg	0.06mg
calcium	510mg	11mg	6mg

Source: Royal Society of Chemistry / Ministry of Agriculture, Fisheries & Food. Information from the supplements to The Composition of Foods is Crown copyright. It is reproduced with the permission of the Controller of Her Majesty's Stationery Office.

Types of tofu

The taste of tofu varies depending on how it is made

Extracting soya milk:

Soya beans are soaked in water, with more water added as it is absorbed. They are then ground, boiled and strained. This strained liquid is soya milk, and the remaining dregs are the tofu lees. The actual soya milk is the main ingredient in tofu.

Momen-dōfu (cotton strained tofu)

This is the traditional tofu that is hard to crumble. A coagulant is added to the soya milk and some of the water is squeezed out and discarded in order to shape the tofu into blocks. It is ideal for cooked dishes.

Kinugoshi-dōfu (silken strained tofu)

This tofu has a softer finer texture, and is often called 'silken tofu'. This is the original Japanese tofu. This is eaten raw.

Yose-dōfu (crumbled tofu)

The method of making this is the same as that of *momen-dōfu*, but after adding the coagulant it isn't shaped into blocks but is sold as it comes. It contains a lot of water and has a soft texture.

Soya bean products

There are a lot of products made from soya beans

There are many nutritious products made from tofu, as well as foods made from the by-products of tofu making.

Tofu processed foods

1. *Abura-age* (thin deep-fried tofu)
   Momen-dōfu sliced and deep-fried.
2. *Atsu-age* (thick deep-fried tofu)
   Momen-dōfu drained and deep-fried.
3. *Ganmodoki* (deep-fried tofu dumpling)
   Momen-dōfu crumbled, drained, filling added then fried like dumplings.
4. *Yaki-dōfu* (grilled tofu)
   Momen-dōfu drained and grilled.
5. *Kori-dōfu* (frozen tofu)
   Frozen to preserve. To eat, defrost and boil.

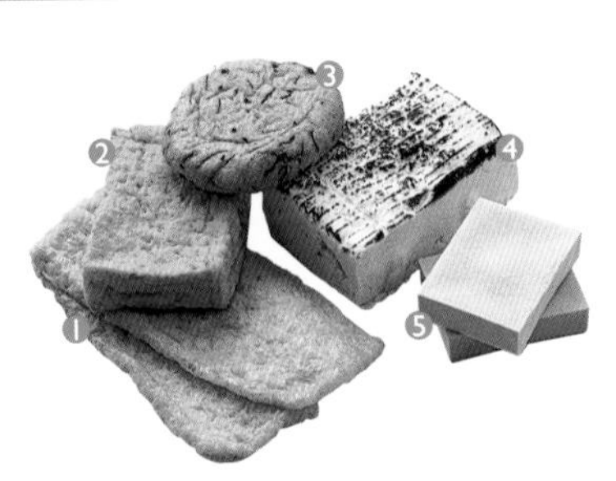

Soya bean processed foods

1. *Tounyu* (soya milk) — Can be drunk hot or cold.
2. *Yuba* (soya milk skin) — The skin that forms on the surface of heated soya milk, used in cooking. Can be dried.
3. *Okara* (tofu lees) — The dregs of boiled soya beans. Makes a good appetiser when cooked with vegetables.

Chilled Tofu

冷やっこ *Hiyayakko*

Serves 1

140g silken tofu ($\frac{1}{2}$ standard size block, strained)

$\frac{1}{4}$ spring onion

$\frac{1}{2}$ *myoga*

small piece fresh ginger

some soy sauce

1. Slice the spring onion and *myoga*, 2-3mm and grate the ginger.

2. Serve the tofu on a plate, garnished with the spring onion, *myoga*, and ginger.

3. Serve with soy sauce.

Simmered Tofu

湯豆腐 *Yu-dōfu*

Serves 4

560g cotton tofu (2 x standard size block, strained)

1 sheet *konbu* 15cm x 15cm

2 spring onions

30g ginger

[A for dipping sauce]

150ml soup stock

130ml soy sauce

75ml *mirin*

1 Make a lot of slits in the *konbu* (cutting in one direction). Cut the tofu into 8 pieces, and slice the spring onions finely, 2mm. Grate the ginger.

2 Place A in a pan and bring it to the boil to make the dipping sauce. Pour the sauce in individual small dipping bowls and add some spring onion and ginger.

3 

Place the *konbu* in a pot (preferably clay) of water, just over half full, and bring it to the boil. Then add the tofu, just as it returns to the boil remove the tofu and dip it in the sauce before eating.

Deep-Fried Tofu with Amber Sauce

● 揚げだし豆腐 *Agedashi-dōfu* ●

These make great party 'nibbles'.

Serves 2

280g cotton tofu (1 standard size block, strained)

some plain flour /cornflour

some vegetable or sunflower oil

5cm *daikon*

1 Wrap the tofu in a tea towel and place something on top of it such as a small bowl to force out excess water, leave the bowl in position for about 15 minutes.

Agedashi-dōfu

1 dried red chilli
some Japanese chives

[A]
2 tbsp soup stock
1 tbsp soy sauce
½ tbsp *mirin*

2 Cut the tofu into 8 even pieces and coat them with flour.

3 

Grate the dried red chilli and radish together.

4 Bring A to the boil to make the sauce.

Agedashi-dōfu

Coat the tofu thoroughly with the flour to ensure even cooking.

5 Deep-fry the tofu until golden brown, and place it on kitchen paper to remove excess oil.

Place the fried tofu on a plate and pour the sauce over and garnish with chopped chives, grated radish and chilli.

Tofu Stewed with Meat and Vegetables

肉豆腐 *Niku-dōfu*

Serves 2

280g cotton tofu (1 standard size block, strained)
150g thinly sliced beef
½ leek
100g *shirataki*

[A]
300ml soup stock
2 tbsp soy sauce
1 tbsp *mirin*

* See page 12 how to drain tofu

1. Cut the drained tofu into 8 pieces, and the beef into bite size pieces.

2. Slice the leek diagonally, 3cm. Cut the *shirataki* into 5cm lengths and cook in boiling water for a few minutes.

3. Place A in a pan and bring it to the boil. Once boiled, add the tofu, beef, leek, and *shirataki* and cook it for 10 minutes on a low heat, and then serve.

Stir-fried Tofu with Chilli Bean Paste

マーボー豆腐 *Mābō-dōfu*

This great spicy recipe really stimulates the appetite.

Serves 4

560g silken tofu
(2 x standard size block, strained)

150g minced pork

1 clove garlic

1 leek

small piece fresh ginger

1 dried red chilli

* See page 12 how to drain tofu

1. Cut the drained tofu into cubes, 2cm.

2. Chop the garlic, the leek, and the ginger.

10g cornflour mixed with 15ml water

½ tsp sesame oil

[A]

80ml Chinese soup stock

1 tbsp Chinese red bean chilli paste

1 tbsp *sake*

1 tbsp sugar

2 tbsp soy sauce

¼ tsp salt

3 Seed the red chilli and slice it finely, 5mm.

4 Heat the sesame oil in a wok, and fry the garlic, leek, and ginger.

5 Add the minced pork and chilli and contine to stir-fry.

Tip!

Don't stir too fiercely once you've added the tofu.

6 Add the tofu and A, and bring to the boil. Cover with a lid and simmer for 10 minutes on a low heat to allow the tofu to soak up the seasoning.

7

Add the cornflour (mixed with the water) to thicken.

Tofu Salad

豆腐サラダ *Tōfu Salada*

Serves 2

280g silken tofu
(1 standard size block, strained)

some lettuce

½ carrot

½ onion

1 tomato

[A]

1 tbsp vegetable or sunflower oil

3 tbsp soy sauce

3 tbsp Japanese vinegar

2 tbsp *mirin*

70ml water

some salt and pepper

1 Separate and break up the lettuce leaves. Cut the carrot finely, 4cm x 2mm. Slice up the onion, 2mm and soak in water. Cut the tomato into wedges.

Mix A in a bowl for the dressing.

3 * See page 12 how to drain tofu

Drain the tofu well and cut it into 6 pieces. Arrange the tofu and salad on plates and pour over the dressing.

Fried Tofu with Vegetables

炒り豆腐 *Iri-dōfu*

Serves 4

280g silken tofu (1 standard size block, strained)
3 *shiitake* mushrooms
½ carrot
2 tbsp garden peas
1 egg
1 tsp sesame oil
½ tbsp vegetable or sunflower oil

[A]

80ml soup stock
3 ½ tbsp soy sauce
1 tbsp sugar
1 tbsp *mirin*
1 tbsp *sake*

* See page 12 how to drain tofu

1. Wrap the drained tofu in a tea towel to remove excess water. Remove the stem of the *shiitake*, and then slice them up with the carrot.

2. Heat both the vegetable oil and sesame oil in a pan and fry the *shiitake* and carrot. Crumble the tofu and add it to the stir-fry. Add A and cook for 5-6 minutes until the sauce is almost reduced to nothing.

3. Just before it's ready pour in the beaten egg, stir, and sprinkle over the garden peas.

Miso Soup with Tofu

豆腐の味噌汁 *Tōfu no Miso-shiru*

Serves 4

140g silken tofu
(½ standard size block, strained)

1 spring onion

40g *miso*

1 litre soup stock

* See page 12 how to drain tofu

1 Cut the tofu into cubes 1.5cm. Slice the spring onion diagonally, 5mm.

Heat up the soup stock for 3-4 minutes and gently dissolve the *miso* in the soup.

3 Add the tofu, heat it gently, taking care that it doesn't come to a boil. Garnish with spring onion just before serving.

Tofu with Savoury Sauce

あんかけ豆腐 *Ankake-dōfu*

Serves 4

280g cotton tofu (1 standard size block, strained)

½ chicken thigh

60g carrot

4 *shiitake* mushrooms

60g *shungiku*

10g cornflour mixed with 15ml water

some grated ginger

[A]

350ml soup stock

4 tbsp *mirin*

3 tbsp soy sauce

* See page 12 how to drain tofu

1. Cut the chicken into bite size pieces, and the carrot 4cm x 3mm. Stem the *shiitake* and slice finely, 3mm.

2. Cook the chicken in a pan with A, the carrots and *shiitake*, on a medium heat. When the chicken is cooked, add the cornflour mixture to thicken.

3. Cut the drained tofu in quarters, and heat it up in another pan with hot water. Remove tofu from the pan, serve it on a plate, and pour the chicken and vegetable sauce over it. Serve with *shungiku* (which have been boiled very quickly, and cut into 4cm length strips) and garnish with the grated ginger.

Tofu Seasoned with Soy Sauce

豆腐なべ照り *Tōfu Nabeteri*

Serves 4

560g cotton tofu
(2 x standard size block, strained)

2 tbsp sesame oil

some plain flour /cornflour

some chives

[A]

2 tbsp soy sauce

4 tbsp *sake*

4 tbsp *mirin*

½ tbsp sugar

* See page 12 how to drain tofu

1 Cut each drained tofu block into 6 thin blocks, and coat them with flour.

2 Heat the sesame oil in a pan and fry the tofu on a medium heat, careful not to touch the tofu, just shaking the pan lightly. Gently brown the tofu, turning them with care.

3 

Add A and continue shaking the pan gently until the tofu is cooked and the sauce has thickened. Serve the tofu on a plate, and garnish with chopped chives.

Oven Baked Tofu

● 犠牲豆腐 *Gisei-dōfu* ●

A very traditional tofu dish with the delicacy of taste that's characteristic of Japanese home cooking.

Serves 4

1,120 g cotton tofu (4 x standard size block, strained)

2 eggs

80g fresh gingko nuts

40g carrot

4 *shiitake* mushrooms

1 tbsp toasted sesame seeds

* See page 12 how to drain tofu

1 Wrap the drained tofu in a tea towel to remove excess water.

2 Grind the tofu with a mortar and pestle (pouring away the water), add the egg and A.

[A]
2 tbsp soy sauce
1 tbsp sugar

3 Peel and boil the gingko nuts, and then slice up thinly.

4 Cut the carrot and the *shiitake* very finely, 2mm, and boil for 3-4 minutes.

Gisei-dōfu

Wrap the tofu in foil in the oven to prevent it from drying out or burning at the edges.

5 Mix all the ingredients together.

6

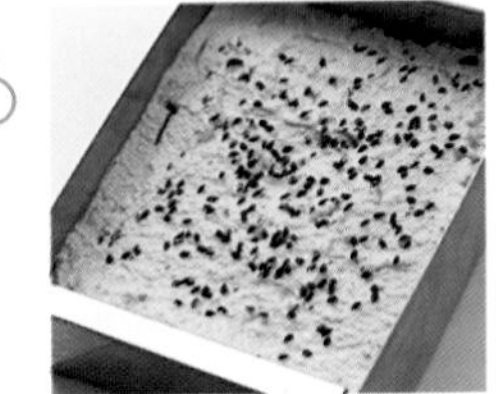

Coat a small roasting tin with oil, pour in the mixture, and flatten the surface. Sprinkle with the toasted sesame seeds and bake it in a preheated oven, 180°C for 5 -10min .

7 Once cooled, cut up and serve.

Tofu with Miso Paste

豆腐田楽 *Tōfu Dengaku*

Serves 4

560g cotton tofu (2 x standard size block, strained)

some dried seaweed flakes

some poppy seeds

[A]

80g white *miso* paste

1 egg yolk

3 ½ tbsp soup stock

1 ½ tbsp *mirin*

1 tbsp sugar

[B]

80g red *miso* paste

1 egg yolk

3 ½ tbsp soup stock

1 ½ tbsp *mirin*

1 tbsp sugar

* See page 12 how to drain tofu

1. Cut each drained tofu block into 6 even pieces, and put each piece on a skewer.

2. Heat A in a pan on low. Heat B in another pan on low and stir.

3. Coat a roasting tin thinly with oil and bake the tofu in a preheated oven, 180°C for 5 minutes. Take the tofu out of the oven, and coat half with A and half with B. Put them back in the oven again, and bake until lightly browned.

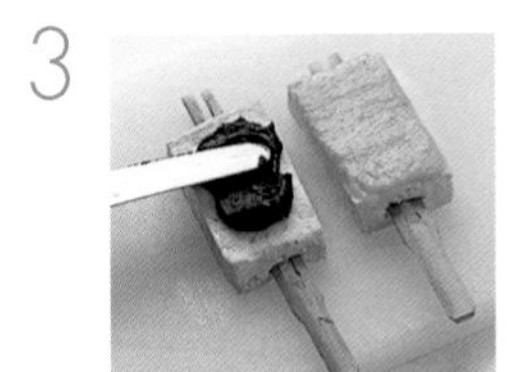

4. Garnish with dried seaweed and poppy seeds.

Ground Tofu with Vegetables

白あえ *Shiroae*

Serves 4

- 280g cotton tofu (1 standard size block, strained)
- 500g *konnyaku*
- ½ carrot
- 4 *shiitake* mushrooms
- 5 tbsp ground white sesame seeds
- 100g spinach

[A]

- 240ml soup stock
- 1 ½ tbsp soy sauce
- 1 ½ tbsp *mirin*

[B]

- 1 tbsp sugar
- 1 tbsp *mirin*
- 1 tbsp *sake*
- 2 ½ tbsp white *miso* paste
- ½ tsp salt
- 2 tbsp soup stock

1. Boil the *konnyaku* and carrot in water for 2 minutes, and then cut them up, 4.5cm x 1cm. Stem the *shiitake* and slice, 3cm.

2. Cook the *konnyaku*, carrot, *shiitake*, and A in a pan until the sauce is reduced to nothing.

3. Wrap the drained tofu in a tea towel to remove excess water. * See page 12 how to drain tofu

Grind the tofu and ground sesame with a mortar and pestle, and add B. Cook the spinach then mix all the ingredients together, and serve.

Tofu Steak

豆腐ステーキ *Tōfu Stēki*

Serves 1

280g cotton tofu (1 standard size block, strained)

100g *shimeji* mushrooms

1 clove garlic

5g butter

1 ½ tbsp soy sauce

1 tbsp *sake*

* See page 12 how to drain tofu

1. Cut the drained tofu into 3 even pieces. Slice the garlic finely, 2mm.

2. Fry the garlic in the butter until browned, and then remove it, and sauté the *shimeji* mushrooms until soft and then remove them.

3. Place the tofu in the pan and fry both sides on a medium heat. Put the garlic back in the pan and add the soy sauce and *sake* as the finishing touch. Serve with the mushrooms.

Tofu Hamburger

豆腐ハンバーグ *Tōfu Hambāgu*

These are ideal for anyone on a diet, as tofu is so low in calories.

Serves 4

280g cotton tofu (1 standard size block, strained)

300g minced beef and pork

½ onion

* See page 12 how to drain tofu

1 Wrap the drained tofu in a tea towel to remove excess water.

Tōfu Hambāgu

[A]

1 egg yolk

15g breadcrumbs

some salt and pepper

1 tsp butter

1 tbsp vegetable or sunflower oil

[B]

120ml ketchup

2 tbsp Worcestershire sauce

some soy sauce

2 Fry the chopped onion in butter and then remove it from the pan and allow to cool.

3 Place the tofu, onion, minced meat, and A in a bowl, and mix thoroughly. It will become quite sticky.

4

Divide the mixture into 4 and shape them into flattened ovals. Make a shallow hollow in the centre of each.

Tōfu Hambāgu

Knead the hamburger mixture thoroughly to remove air, so that the hamburgers don't crumble when fried.

5 Fry the hamburgers on a medium heat, turn when browned on one side, put a lid on and continue frying. When clear juice emerges on the surface of the hamburgers, they are cooked.

Discard the oil from the pan and add B to make the sauce. Bring it to the boil.

7 Serve the hamburgers on plates and pour the sauce over.

Tofu Croquette

豆腐コロッケ *Tōfu Korokke*

Serves 4

280g cotton tofu (1 standard size block, strained)

150g minced beef

½ onion

6 *shiso* leaves

some plain flour

1 beaten egg

some breadcrumbs

some vegetable or sunflower oil

[A]

½ egg

1 tbsp soy sauce

some salt

* See page 12 how to drain tofu

1. Wrap the drained tofu in a tea towel to remove excess water. Mash the tofu with A. Stem the *shiso* leaves, and cut finely, 2mm, and mix them in with the tofu.

2. Fry the chopped onion, and then add the minced beef. Once cooked, remove them from the pan and add to the tofu mixture.

3. Shape the mixture into 8 small balls, and then coat each in flour, beaten egg, and breadcrumbs consecutively. Deep-fry them until the surface is browned. Use kitchen paper to remove excess oil.

• Guide to ingredients - Tofu •

Daikon	—	Japanese radish
Dashi	—	Japanese soup stock
Gin-nan	—	ginkgo nuts
Konbu	—	kelp
Konnyaku	—	vegetarian jelly made from devil's tongue plant
Mirin	—	cooking sake (sweet)
Miso	—	fermented soya bean paste
Myoga	—	Japanese ginger
Nori	—	sheet of dried seaweed – 'standard size' refers to sheet: 21cm x 19 cm
Osu	—	Japanese vinegar
Sake	—	Japanese rice wine
Shiitake	—	variety of mushroom
Shimeji	—	small brown-topped mushrooms
Shirataki	—	thin konnyaku noodles
Shiso	—	beefsteak plant
Shungiku	—	edible chrysanthemum leaves